Dandelion Tea
in a Weedy World

Learning to See God's Love
with Mirror Poems and Ink

Janet K. Gardner

WESTBOW
PRESS®
A DIVISION OF THOMAS NELSON
& ZONDERVAN

WestBow Press books may be ordered through booksellers or by contacting:

WestBow Press
A Division of Thomas Nelson & Zondervan
1663 Liberty Drive
Bloomington, IN 47403
www.westbowpress.com
844-714-3454

Because of the dynamic nature of the Internet, any web addresses or links contained in this book may have changed since publication and may no longer be valid. The views expressed in this work are solely those of the author and do not necessarily reflect the views of the publisher, and the publisher hereby disclaims any responsibility for them.

Janet's "JG Anchor-Cross" signature mark and "Janet Gardner Inspirations" are trademarks of Janet K. Gardner.

For poetic emphasis and Mirror Poem structure, capitalization, italics, line breaks, and centering have been added as needed to scripture quotations.

For poetic clarity, proper names have been inserted for their corresponding pronouns. Quotations without translation references are paraphrased from the original Scripture.

Some illustrations parody works by other artists:
"Blooming in Love" is a parody of "The Scream" (1893) by Edvard Munch,
"Embracing the Son" is a parody of "The Creation of Adam" (1512) by Michelangelo.

Readers may follow or message Janet K. Gardner on
Facebook @JanetGardnerInspirations.

Framed images and printed gifts of Janet's artwork are available from
www.FineArtAmerica.com as "Janet K. Gardner Inspirational."

ISBN: 978-1-6642-7329-0 (sc)
ISBN: 978-1-6642-7330-6 (e)

Library of Congress Control Number: 2022913468

Print information available on the last page.

WestBow Press rev. date: 08/12/2022

Dedication and Gratitude

For those searching for something …
because on some days we are the sheep,
and other days a shepherd!

For the young and old …
because we want on some days to read about God's love,
and on other days
just to look at the pictures.

And with deepest gratitude to:

Mom, who first told me of God's love in stories with puppets;
Dad, who showed me God's love by baking bread and smoking fish;
Robert, who reflects God's love by putting up with me;
John, who reminds me of God's love by not telling his dad what really happened;
John August Swanson, who graciously reviewed the early drafts of this book
but returned to our Father before its formal printing;
Ascension Lutheran Church for continuing to nourish my heart with God's love;
Reverend Dr. Paul and Jean Gravrock for their editing and theological advice;
Reverend Dr. Tim Delkeskamp for his spiritual guidance and shepherding;
Reverend Dr. Jack and Dolores Ledbetter for their poetic friendships over the decades;
Pastors Steve Herder and Julie McCain for their support and guidance;
WestBow's design team, staff, and my editor, Cynthia, for their support and vision;
And most of all to my Heaven Father,
who's been patiently growing this amazing book with me all my life!

Contents

List of Illustrations

Introduction: Reflections on Mirror Poetry

What is a "mirror poem"?

Simply stated, a mirror poem is prose with a reflective heart, for its ending half spiritually reflects and echoes its beginning half. But like ripples over still water, these halves rarely match exactly, word for word. Sometimes, only a key word or its rhyming twin echoes. Other times it's a perfect match word for word. Intentionally, the lines are centered, and the second half will often look deeper or explain the upper part. Other times it completes the story or raises a prayer for the struggles depicted in the first half.

In a mirror poem, italic lines are not directly mirrored. They are transitional lines between the mirroring phrases. Their purpose is to move the poem along while adding clarity, depth, and meaning.

In the middle of each mirror poem is the literal center that reveals its key theme and focus. As such, it is the poem's heart and a bridge connecting its beginning with its reflective ending. For these poems, that focus is Jesus! With His many names at each poem's center, we are reminded that we too should keep Him centered in our lives.

How do I read a mirror poem?

As with prose or conventional poems, a mirror poem is read first from beginning to end but may be reread to gain more meaning and depth. But from there, a mirror poem is unique in offering another perspective into its imagery. When reading from the center out, one alternates between the top and bottom parts to purposely find the mirroring lines. Italic lines, while read separately, should not be skipped but read as a side note. In this center-out reading, emphasis is placed on the similarities and differences between the reflecting lines. Sometimes they are an exact match, but usually there are differences such as added words or variants on rhyming words. In a few poems, the last line even mirrors the title.

Haiku appear on the title pages that divide the mirror poems into three parts. While traditional haiku are written to stand alone, these are grouped to tell three little "stories" and, as with "Shepherding Haiku," to add some light humor as well.

Reflections on the Illustrations

An artist's work changes over time—especially mine!

During the years writing and painting *Dandelion Tea*, my painting style evolved to reflect my personal walk with God.

In 2018 I began the earliest ink drawings with sword and fan brushes. My first illustration was the image of the lost sheep for "Repenting," with its simple brush strokes depicting a detailed scene. Some of the more complex pictures, as for the poems "Blooming in Love," "Gardening," and "Raging," required pencil sketches. The image for "Following the Shepherd" was the segue to the next series of images depicting hands for the poems "Embracing," "Drawing Water," "Praying," "Crying Out," and "Doubting" and the feet for "Running." Sketching out each image took more time. Paintings that began simply grew more and more complicated.

Then everything changed. It happened one day while painting and then wiping my brush onto a nearby piece of paper. To my amazement, I unintentionally made the simple, spontaneous brush strokes that resulted in the image *Crucifixion without Thought* on page 50. It is one of my favorite paintings, and its simplicity prompted me to redirect my brush work to a more minimalist style like that of the Japanese sumi-e painters.

So then I began painting bamboo and sheep—lots of them! My travels to Maui and hiking through its lush rainforests inspired even more bamboo images. At this same time, I adopted the simple but dramatic use of painting with pure drops of India ink onto a wet image. All of *Traveling with the Shepherd* on page xiv was painted like this, as well as a few of the images for the reflection questions. Yosemite and Half Dome also inspired many of the mountain illustrations and no doubt will be an ongoing theme for places depicting God's awesome majesty.

As for symbolism, the shepherd images represent Jesus the Shepherd, of course, but also today's shepherding leader guiding students, for even a sheep will eventually become a shepherd to someone. The three birds in many of the pictures represent the Trinity. The dandelion pictures quietly show cross-carrying seeds and the secret crosses among bamboo groves and mountains act as reminders that God's love is always there for us, even if it seems hidden. For truly "now we see only a reflection, as in a mirror; then we shall see face to face" (1 Corinthians 13:12a NIV).

Mirror Prayer for Illumination

O Lord, where is my strength, O Redeemer,
To write, paint, and read these prayerful poems?
And will they be acceptable in Thy sight,
These meditations of my heart,
Soul-searching shadows of brush and pen,
Like the weary words of my mouth?

CHRIST THE LORD!

"Let the words of my mouth,
And the meditations of my heart,
Be acceptable in thy sight,
O LORD, my strength and my redeemer."

Psalm 19:14 KJV

Amen.

Part 1

Seeing God in a Weedy World

Jesus put before them another parable:
"The Kingdom of Heaven may be compared
to someone who sowed good seed in his field;
but while everybody was asleep,
an enemy came and sowed weeds among the wheat,
and then went away." (Matthew 13:24 NRSV)

Gardening

Haiku

Turned, earthy soil,
thorned weeds sprout with righteous wheat.
God's love waters all.

Our Gardener waits,
for pulling weeds uproots all.
Good sprouts now struggle.

Harvest day arrives:
bread bakes, weeds burn, as tea steeps:
Dandelion songs!

God Is Nowhere

Hopeless!
I give up, choking on a charred future.
For everywhere I see harm:
Another shooting!
Suicide!
Cancer!
Burnt, muddy, broken homes!
Abuse of others, drugs, and alcohol!
My warm, fuzzy plans grow gummy like seat-cushion bus fare,
For I, too, have lost You, O Lord!
And surely I think I know my plans …
But I don't.
Help me!

SAVIOR!

Helping me:
"'For surely I know the plans
I have for you,' says the LORD,
'Plans for your welfare
And not for harm,
To give you a future
With hope.'"

Jeremiah 29:11 NRSV

God is now here!

Repenting

"Have mercy on me, O God,
According to your unfailing love;
According to your great compassion,
Blot out my transgressions.
Wash away all my iniquity
And cleanse me from my sin.

Create in me a clean heart, O God,
And renew a right spirit within me.
Cast me not away from your presence
And take not your Holy Spirit from me.
Restore to me the joy of your salvation
And uphold me with a willing spirit."

Psalm 51:1b–2, 10–12 NIV

REDEEMER!

Truly, I am a lost sheep!

Psalm 119:176a KJV

On Your shepherding shoulders,
Uphold me with Your filling Spirit,
Rescue me with the joy of Your salvation,
And don't fence off Your Holy Spirit from me.
Lead me not astray from Your presence,
But come and find me,
And renew a leaping-lamb spirit within me
For I am scared, alone, and trembling with fear.
Create in me a clean, repenting heart, O God,
For in my sin, I am truly lost!

Find and cleanse me from my sins.
"Wash me and I will be whiter than snow."

Psalm 51:7b NIV

In the soothing waters of Your Spirit,
Wash away all my wickedness.
In Your blood, blot out the stains of my transgressions,
For according to Your love, great is Your compassion,
And according to Your compassion, unfailing is Your love,
All for me, a lost sheep, in the wilderness.
Have mercy on me, O God!
Come and find me!

Amen.

Groaning

Heavenly Father,
Saving Son,
Hear our cries,
Tears,
Sobs and sighs,
Wordless groans!
Intercede for us,
Holy Spirit, Ever-Present Self,
For You know what we pray for
In our weakness.
Come our way, Holy Spirit! Help us!

HOLY ONE!

"In the same way, the Spirit helps us
In our weakness.
We do not know what we ought to pray for,
But the Spirit himself
Intercedes for us
With wordless groans."

Romans 8:26 NIV

Amen.

Smothering Fires

Is God still our fortress when the forests flame?
Is our loving Lord Almighty still with us
When smoke and ash are exalted by earth's fires?
For this torching cannot be halted among the nations,
Refusing to be still and let go. Hear and know us, ever-loving God!
For hatred now burns our fields with fire
And breaks our hearts and shatters our hopes.
Who can make our searing wars cease to the ends of the earth,
These charred desolations brought against the earth?
Come and see what we have done,
And then pray: "Forgive us, God! Be again our fortress!"
Does our Lord Almighty still love us?
Again and again, mountains quake and burn with surging ash.
From aching eyes, our tears choke us and water our roar
But fail to quench the mountain's flames as our hoping hearts fall into the sea.
As we boil over with fear, see how the earth gasps and gives way!
Who is our refuge and strength? Where is our loving, ever-present help in these troubles?

CAPTAIN OF SALVATION!

"God is our refuge and strength, an ever-present help in trouble.
Therefore, we will not fear though the earth gives way,
And the mountains fall into the heart of the sea.
Though its waters roar and foam
And the mountains quake with their surging.
The Lord Almighty is with us;
The God of Jacob is our fortress.
Come and see what the Lord has done,
Who has brought desolations in the earth.
He makes wars cease to the ends of the earth.
He breaks the bow and shatters the spear;
He burns the shields with fire.
He says, 'Be still [let go!], and know that I am God;
I will be exalted among the nations,
I will be exalted in the earth.'
The Lord Almighty is with us;
The God of Jacob is our fortress."

Psalm 46:1–3, 7–11 NIV

Drawing Water

The drought years hit us hard
When the news crushed God's name like dried leaves
And dared us to proclaim His name exalted,
While making its own deeds known among the nations.
For droughts don't give thanks to the Lord or call upon His name!
And who will say on that dark, dusty day
Who can show us the Way
To the wells of salvation?
Or how from joyless tears do you draw water?
So what has become of our salvation?
Is the news now an adored god? To itself, it is strength and might.
Or whom now will we trust when we are so afraid
Of dying dry?
Surely, God, who will bring salvation?

IMMANUEL!

"Surely God is my salvation;
I will trust, and will not be afraid,
For the Lord God is my strength and my might;
He has become my salvation.
With joy you will draw water
From the wells of salvation.
And you will say on that day:
Give thanks to the Lord, call on His name;
Make known His deeds among the nations;
Proclaim His name exalted."

Isaiah 12:2–4 NRSV

Blooming in Love

"Love is patient; love is kind.
It does not envy, it does not boast, it is not proud.
It does not dishonor others, it is not self-seeking,
It is not easily angered, it keeps no record of wrongs.
Love does not delight in evil but rejoices with the truth.
Love bears all things, believes all things,
Hopes all things, endures all things.
Love never ends."

1 Corinthians 13:4–6 NIV; 7–8a WEB

LORD OF ALL!

Whose love never ends,
Forgive us! Repot our tangled roots and withering faith in Your love.
For we trellis our hopes to all worldly things, while Your love endures all things.
Truly, Your love bears all things so that we may believe in all You bring.
You don't delight in evil but rejoice in love and truth!
Although we are easily angered, O God, Your love keeps no record of our wrongs,
For Your Son "was pierced for our transgressions.
He was crushed for our iniquities;
The punishment that brought our Peace was on Him,
And by His wounds we are healed."

Isaiah 53:5 WEB

Through Your love,
You honor us and others, although we are self-seeking,
Undeserving with weeds of envy and boasting pride.
Repot us in Your love, O Lord, and we shall bloom patient and kind.

Amen

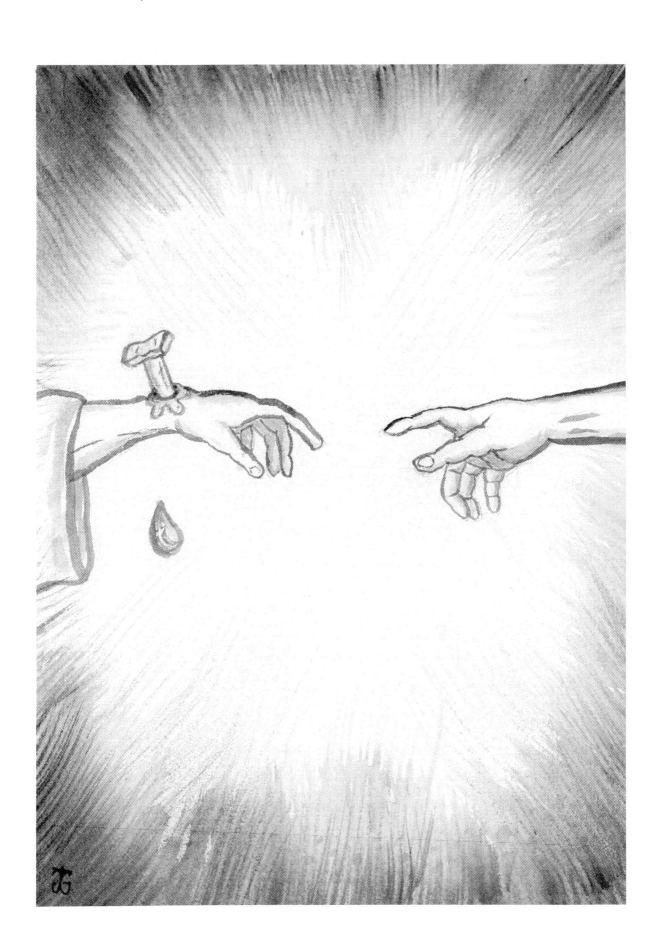

Embracing

"For God so loved the World,
That He gave His only begotten Son,
That whoever believes in Him
Shall not perish
But have eternal life."

John 3:16 NASB

SON OF GOD!

Through Your ever-washing waves of grace,
I have eternal life
And shall not perish
In the stinking, stagnant pools of my sin,
Pulling me under into a trashy tomb—a discarded cross!—
Of moldy bread, spoiled wine, and unsung psalms,
My abandoned Communion with You!
But I must believe in You, Lord Jesus,
Believe that our Father gave up You—His only begotten Son!—
Discarded
To die on my own rotting cross,
A cross handmade by me, for me!
Truly, for those of us believing,
How You save us is not important,
Just why:
Why steal my decaying cross—and compost it?
Why embrace our garage heaps—and grow flowers?
For God so loved the entire world,
Embracing!

Ever Shining

"In the beginning was the Word,
And the Word was with God,
And the Word was God.
He was in the beginning with God.
All things came into being through Him,
And without Him not one thing came into being.
What has come into being in Him was life,
And the life was the Light of all people.
The Light shines in the darkness,
And the darkness did not overcome it."

John 1:1–5 NRSV

WORD OF GOD!

The darkest storms cannot overcome You, O Lord,
My Light, ever shining over the pounding waves of darkness,
For You are my life and the Light of all people.
Truly in You, O Lord, is life!
For without You, not one thing can come into being.
Even the raging seas are Yours!
Truly, all things came into being through You.
For You were there in the beginning with God,
Ever calming over the wrecking waves of chaos,
For You, O Lord, are the Word, and God
The Verb,
Ever moving,
Ever creating
Over the roaring waters of our lives.
Yes! You are the Word with God
From the beginning and now with redeeming words,
Ever loving!
Ever shining!

Running

"So then let us rid ourselves
Of everything that gets in the way,
And of sin which holds on to us so tightly,
And let us run with determination
The race that lies before us.
Let us keep our eyes fixed on Jesus,
On whom our faith depends
From beginning to end."

Hebrews 12:1b–2a GNT

ALPHA AND OMEGA!

You are
The Beginning and the End,
The now and always
On whom my faith all depends,
So that I may keep my eyes fixed on You, Lord Jesus,
As I run this race that lies before me.
Help me, Lord,
To run with patient determination
Against my sins, which hold on to me tightly,
Pulling me down,
Ruining everything, and getting in the way
Like tangling weeds,
Tripping me as we run together.
Help me, Lord!
Rid me of everything
That blocks me from seeing Your endless love—
Love that is now and always
Running!

Amen

Fluttering

"Ask the animals, and they will teach you;
Ask the birds of the air, and they will tell you;
Or speak to the earth, and it will instruct you;
Let the fish of the sea inform you.
Which of all these does not know
That the hand of the LORD has done this?
That the life of every living thing is in His hand,
As well as the breath of all mankind."

Job 12:7–10 NIV

"The grass withers,
The flower fades;
But the Word of our God
Stands forever."

Isaiah 40:8 WEB

GLORY OF THE LORD!

It should have stood forever,
That old pine in Pastor's yard.
It should have lived like the Word of our God,
But it died that one blazing summer
As its pinecones, like flowers, faded and fell,
As its needles withered like dry grass.
But that death was three years ago,
And now a new breath, the all-loving kind,
Swirls around new, greening growth,
Reminding us that the life of every living thing is in His hands.
Yes! The hand of our Lord has done this.
For sweet passion-fruit flowers now vine up wrinkled bark,
And where death once yawned and lounged,
Monarch butterflies now flutter upon God's passionate hand.
So now all may know
A dead tree's secret: to look for God's love in His creations.
For the fish of the sea will inform you
God's love is ever flowing,
And speak to the earth, for it will instruct you
God's love is boundless!
Then ask the birds of the air, and they will tell you
God's love is forever free!
Then lastly ask the animals, and they will teach you
God's love is alive
And saved a sinner like me,
A dead tree now budding with fragrant flowers and butterflies
Fluttering!

Soaring

"But those who trust in the LORD
Will find new strength.
They will soar high on wings like eagles.
They will run and not grow weary.
They will walk and not faint."

Isaiah 40:31 NLT

Sleepy hills of winter
Yawn with sprouting green,
Awakened by caressing rains
And uplifting breaths
Over still wings
Of dancing eagles
Ever trusting
That the breeze
Will lift them higher.

SUN OF RIGHTEOUSNESS!

You, O Lord, will lift us higher
On Your breeze
Ever loving!
So too we dance like eagles
With still, trusting wings
Upon Your uplifting breath.
Come Holy Spirit!
Awaken caressing rains!
Yawn no more, sprouting green!
For in You, O Lord, our wings now trust
And no longer need to flap
Over the sleepy hills of winter,
Soaring!

"But unto you that fear My name
Shall the Sun of Righteousness arise
With healing in His wings."

Malachi 4:2a KJV

Climbing Mountains

"A song of ascents.
I lift up my eyes to the mountains—
Where does my help come from?
My help comes from the LORD,
The Maker of heaven and earth.

"He will not let your foot slip—
He who watches over you will not slumber;
Indeed, he who watches over Israel
Will neither slumber nor sleep.

*"The LORD watches over you—
The LORD is your shade at your right hand;
The sun will not harm you by day,
Nor the moon by night.*

"The LORD will keep you from all harm—
He will watch over your life;
The LORD will watch over your coming and going
Both now and forevermore."

Psalm 121 NIV

THE WAY!

Now and forevermore,
The Lord will watch over my coming and going.
He will watch over my life
As promised.
The Lord will keep me from all harm,
For He is my Way up life's mountain.

My Lord will neither slumber nor sleep,
And indeed watches over all His people
As promised.
He who watches over me will never slumber;
He will never let my foot slip
*Into Hell's darkest hole, for He is my Way
Up, ever guiding me over life's slippery rocks.*

The Maker of heaven and earth,
My Helper, my Lord, showers me with His love
As promised.
So if you ask me, "Where does my help come from?"
I will reply with a glance,
Lifting my eyes up to the mountains,
*For He is my Way
Up and ascending like a song!*

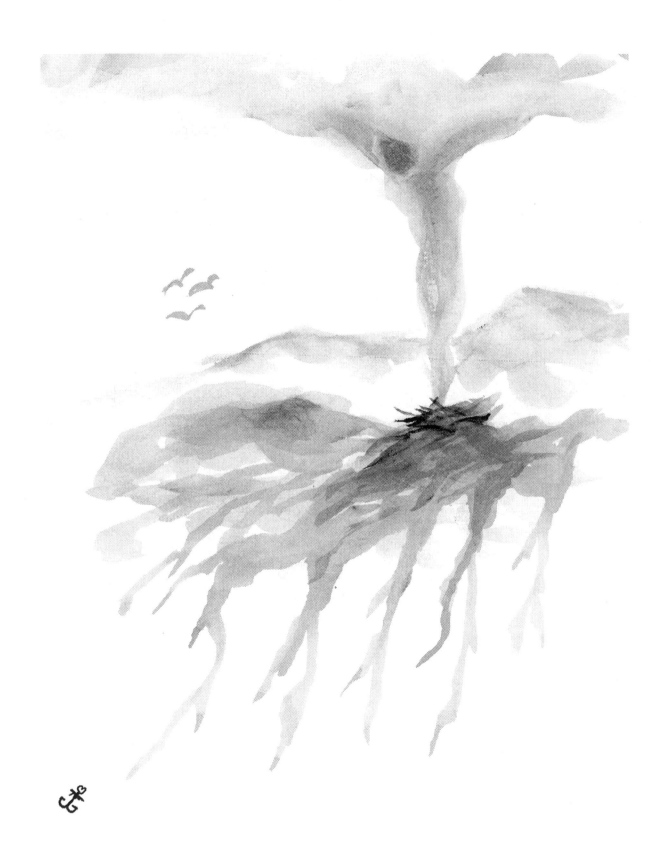

Ever Trusting

Paraphrasing Genesis 22:2, 6–8

Then God said to Abraham,
"Take your son, your only son,
Whom you love, and offer him
There as a sacrifice."
So Abraham took the wood for the sacrifice
And laid it on his son, Isaac, to carry.
Then Isaac said to his father, Abraham,
"Father! Where is the lamb
For the sacrifice?"
Ever trusting and faithful to God,
Abraham replied, "God himself will provide."

Lamb of God!

In Jesus, God himself has provided
The sacrifice
For our sins.
Yes, Father, He is your lamb,
Like Isaac, the only son of Father Abraham,
For now all sins are laid on God's son, Jesus, to carry
With the wood for the cross.
There, O suffering sacrifice,
He whom You love, Father God—You offered Him,
Jesus,
Your Son, Your only Son,
For the sins of all of us.
Help us, O God, to be like Abraham,
Ever trusting!

Amen.

*"But God proves his love for us
In that while we still were sinners
Christ died for us."*

Romans 5:8 NRSV

Following the Shepherd

"The Lord is my shepherd; I shall not want.
He maketh me to lie down in green pastures:
He leadeth me beside still waters.
He restoreth my soul:
He leadeth me in the paths of righteousness
For His name's sake.
Yea though I walk through the valley
Of the shadow of death,
I will fear no evil for thou art with me
Thy rod and thy staff, they comfort me.
Thou preparest a table before me
In the presence of mine enemies:
Thou anointest my head with oil;
My cup runneth over.
Surely goodness and mercy shall follow me
All the days of my life:
And I will dwell in the house of the Lord for ever."

Psalm 23 KJV

Good Shepherd!

I will dwell in the love of my heavenly Lord forever,
All the days of my life,
For His goodness and mercy shall always pursue me
So that my cup runs over
With hidden blessings now and forever.
To blot out the stink of sin,
He anoints me with fragrant oil,
Myrrh from His beloved Son's birth and death,
A stench to my ever-present enemies,
Then prepares a banquet table and feeds all sinners—even me!
My Shepherd's love is truly endless.
His rod guides me as His staff protects me—ready to strike!
I no longer fear evil, for my Shepherd is with me,
And death is now but a shadow of its old self,
For my Good Shepherd now walks through its valley with me.
For His name's sake and glory,
My path now leads to righteousness,
For He has restored my sin-infested soul
And leads me still to renewing waters of the Holy Spirit,
And feeds me, sprawling on His green-nurturing Word—even in rocky desert pastures.
Truly, O God, you are my Shepherd—in You I want nothing else!

Part 2

Seeing God in His Loving Son

My sheep hear my voice,
and I know them, and they follow me:
and I give unto them eternal life;
and they shall never perish,
and no one shall snatch them
out of my hand. (John 10:27–28 ASV)

The Shepherd

Haiku

Sunrise meadow glows.
Dewy wool warms yawning sheep.
Shepherd sips green tea.

Golden greening grass,
another meadow beckons.
Greedy mouths now drool.

Sheep wander away,
rocky gorge along their path.
Golden grass now blinds them.

Warnings unheeded.
Lambs slip into the ravine,
their tomb! Where is God?

Stones fall. Boulder rolls.
Shepherd's hands now stretch and bleed.
Embraced! Lambs rejoice!

Sunset meadow dims.
Tangled wool warms yawning sheep.
Shepherd chugs red wine!

Wielding the Word

paraphrasing Matthew 4:1–11; 6:9–13

Seemingly forever,
For forty days in the wilderness,
Satan battles Jesus, challenging:
"For all the world's kingdoms, powers, and glory,
If you are God's redeeming Son,
Command the angels to deliver You up from my evil,
Leading You into temptation."
But Jesus, wielding the Word, blocks with Deuteronomy 6:16.
"It is written," He proclaims, "Do not put the LORD your God to the test!"
Then again Satan tempted our Lord, hungry and fasting:
"Change this rock to give you your daily bread."
"No. For one does not live by bread alone,"
Parries Jesus with Deuteronomy 8:3,
"But by every Word from the mouth of God!"
They then soar to mountain heights.
On earth but never in heaven,
Satan's will is done
As he shows off his kingdoms now and yet to come:
"All of these I will give you if you worship me,
Proclaiming my name holy
In heaven
Over your Father's!"
But Jesus crushes Satan with Deuteronomy 6:13, His black-eye blow:
"Worship the Lord your God and serve only Him!"

TEACHER!

Prepares us too for battle, praying:
Our Father
In heaven
Holy is Your name.
Your kingdom come,
Your will be done,
On earth as it is in heaven.
Give us this day our daily bread
And forgive us our sins as we forgive those who sin against us.
Lead us not into temptation,
But deliver us from evil
For You are the kingdom, and the power, and the glory—
Forever!

Amen.

Fishing

paraphrasing Luke 5:1–11

An oil lamp flickers on a sycamore bough
Over dark, still waters
Rippling to reflect a beckoning flame,
Flowing through tired knots on empty nets
Among our hungry hearts.
Oh man! No fish! Again, no fish! How come?
A new wick is cut and raised.
With it, our hopes are relit too:
Ah, a brighter light over dark waters!
A piercing light through our gloom.
Now the fish will come!
So again we wait and wait and wait
As the evening stars fade
With the warming glow of morning.
But still, there are no fish!

LIGHT OF THE WORLD!

But now there are fish
With the warming glow of morning.
Our evening hungers faded
As we ate and ate and ate.
Oh, how the fish have come!
With our Lord in our boat,
He is now our Light,
A piercing Light through our gloom!
Ah, a brighter Light over our dark waters!
In Him, our hopes are relit too.
And like a wick, He too will be cut and raised
Someday, all for our sake.
Oh, the men! Like fish. Again like fish! They come
With hungry hearts,
Flowing with tired knots and empty nets
Now rippling to reflect God's Beckoning Flame,
His only Son,
Over dark, still waters,
For we too now shine for Him like
Oil lamps flickering on a sycamore bough.

Prodigal Repenting

paraphrasing Luke 15:1–2, 11–32

One day, standing near Jesus,
Angry Pharisees muttered,
"This man can't be from God. He welcomes sinners and eats with them!"
To this the Teacher sighed, and told them this story.
The youngest of two brothers once said to their wealthy father,
"Father, although it's not your time,
Grant me my birthright now,
Righteously, for there are places to see and things to do."
Overwhelmed with love, his father relented and faithfully gave him his portion.
Immediately, this younger, prodigal son left for distant lands,
Where he spent everything,
Squandering it on lavish living.
A famine then devoured the country so severely that
He hired himself out to feed swine,
Unclean pigs, unclean like sinners.
Soon he yearned to eat something,
Even the rot-bread of their slop,
For salvation can take many forms.
Hopeless and hungry away from home, repenting,
He prayed for help.

BREAD OF LIFE!

He prayed, and help came.
Hopeful, his hunger returned him home—repenting!
For salvation can take many forms,
Even in craving hot bread slopped onto servant plates.
But oh, how the father yearned to see him,
His young, prodigal son, unclean like a pig, a sinner!
Shocking the neighbors, the father ran to him—rejoicing!—
And called his hirelings out to pour wine,
Replace the son's robes and ring, and to kill the fattened calf,
For the sadness that once devoured the country so severely
Was now squandered away by the father's lavish love—
Forgiving everything!
Immediately, the older, pharisaical son left the field lands and returned.
Overwhelmed with anger, he never relented against his unfaithful brother:
"Righteously, father, I've farmed your places and fixed your things,
But you never granted me a party with mirth for the right I've done."
But the father replied, "Although it's his time now for rejoicing,
You have always had my love. Rejoice! For your brother, who was lost, is found!"

Branching Out

"I am the vine; you are the branches.
If you remain in me and I in you,
You will bear much fruit;
Apart from me you can do nothing,"

John 15:5 NIV

Proclaimed our Lord to His disciples
As they gleaned the fallen grapes,
Fruiting grapes that once hung on branches
With ever-seeking tendrils
Clinging to anything:
Fish nets. Passovers. Olive jugs.
Once lost and desperate,
Grape branches and tendrils finally return home,
To their ever-present vine!

Messiah!

To our ever-present Vine, O Lord,
We too, like grape branches, seek to return home to You
For we are lost and desperate.
To the internet, overpasses, and coffee mugs,
We too cling to anything
With ever-seeking tendrils,
But now support the fruits of His labor:
"Love, joy, peace, patience, kindness,
Goodness, faithfulness, gentleness, and self-control,"

Galatians 5:22b–23a WEB

Fruiting as grapes that now hang on our branches,
Once gleaned and fallen
But now proclaiming our Lord to today's disciples:
"Apart from Him we can do nothing.
We will bear much fruit,
If we remain in Him, for His love is in us.
He is our vine and we are His branches—
His hands!"

Amen.

Raging

paraphrasing John 2:13–22

Raging,
Outcasts and the poor
Once filled the temple courtyard,
Now busy with merchants who cry out,
"Too poor to pay? Go away! Gentiles too!
But come out, Jews! Ring bells! Our Father's house has a market!
Send in the lambs running, and the pigeons flying!
Turn coins into whipped rams for sacrifice!"
Wow, the moneychangers charge fiercely!

LAMB OF GOD!

But now our Teacher charges in fiercely,
Turning coins and tables, whipping all—O God's Ram of Sacrifice!—
Sending the other lambs running and pigeons flying.
"Get out, ewes!" He yells. "Our Father's house is not a market!"
Now the poor can pray. Come His way! Gentiles too!
For in Him you pray to God, for He is your temple now!
And He is never too busy for us sinners, like merchants crying out
But now filled with love from His temple courtyards,
Uplifting all outcasts and the poor
With His love
Raging!

Rejoicing

"Rejoice in the Lord always.
Again, I say: Rejoice!
Let your gentleness be known to all …
The Lord is at hand.
In nothing be anxious,
But in everything, by prayer and petition,
With thanksgiving, let your requests be made known to God.
And the peace of God,
Which surpasses all understanding,
Will guard your hearts and your thoughts
In Christ Jesus."

Philippians 4:4–7 WEB

paraphrasing Mark 4:35–41

PRINCE OF PEACE!

Come! Help!
In a rocking boat on a thundering sea,
We cry out with the disciples,
Come, Christ Jesus!
Guard our hearts and thoughts,
You, who surpass all understanding—
Come!
Peace of God!
Come!
And yet we fail,
When we live without thanksgiving and request presents from You, O God.
And yet, in everything, by prayer and petition,
Our Lord is with us in our boat,
Calming our raging seas, while whispering,
"In nothing be anxious,
For your Lord God is near to guide your hand!"
Come!
See how He rebukes the storm!
Commanding it—and us—into calm, calling,
"Let your gentleness be known to all!"
So that we—with the waves—may together
Again say, "Rejoice!
Rejoice in the Lord always!
Rejoice!"

Weeping

paraphrasing John 11:21, 25–26a, 35

For Lazarus, we wept:
"If you were here, Lord,
He would not have died."
Lazarus, who no longer lives and yet believed in Thee,
Christ, Eternal Life.
Then Jesus answered,
"I am ...

THE RESURRECTION!

"I am
The Life!
Those who believe in me, even though they die, will live.
Everyone who lives and believes in me
Will never die."
Then Lazarus rose—and so shall we!
For You are always here, Lord.
For us, Jesus wept!

Praying

paraphrasing Luke 22:39–48

Love is forever, an ever-amen!
Jesus in Gethsemane's garden,
A kingdom of twisted olive trees towering with God's power and glory,
Prays for Judas not to deliver Him to evil,
Evil, richly robed in greed
That leads Judas into temptation.
Yet Jesus forgives his sin against Him,
Just as the Father forgives our sins.
Like freshly baked daily bread
Lovingly given to us each day,
Jesus prays the Psalms, songs sung on earth as they are in heaven.
So too Your will, O Father, be done,
For "Your kingdom is an everlasting kingdom."

Psalm 145:13a NIV

And wow! "How majestic [and Holy!] is Your name …
You have set Your glory in the heavens,"

Psalm 8:1 NIV

Our Father,
Who taught us to pray our Lord's Prayer
Through Your

BELOVED SON!

Our Father
Who art in heaven
Holy is Your name.
Your kingdom come;
Your will be done
On earth as it is in heaven.
Give us this day
Our daily bread
And forgive us our sins
As we forgive those who sin against us.
Lead us not into temptation
But deliver us from evil,
For You are the kingdom, and the power, and the glory
Forever and ever. Amen.

paraphrasing Matthew 6:9–13

Crying Out

To their prophet Samuel,
The Israelites cried out:
"We are determined to have a king over us,
So that we also may be like other nations,
And that our king may govern us,
And go out before us,
And fight our battles!"

1 Samuel 8:19b–20 NRSV

KING OF KINGS!

Jesus,
Fighting our battles,
Going out before us,
Our King who governs us with love,
So that we may not be like others
Determined to have earthly things ruling over us.
But there was a time
When the Jews cried out
Against their prophetic Immanuel:
"Crucify him! Crucify him!"
And Pilate asked, "Shall I crucify your king?"
But the Chief Priests answered,
"We have no king but Caesar!"
Then Pilate handed Him over to be crucified ...
And had an inscription written
And nailed to His cross:
"Jesus of Nazareth, King of the Jews."

paraphrasing John 19:15–19

Prophesying

"When the soldiers had crucified Jesus,
They took His clothes and divided them into four parts,
One for each soldier. They also took His tunic;
Now the tunic was seamless, woven in one piece from the top.
So they said to one another,
'Let us not tear it, but cast lots for it to see who will get it.'"

John 19:23–24a NRSV

So they cast lots for His clothing,
And divided His garments among themselves,
While people looked and stared at Him,
For they could count all His bones, unbroken,
And nails pierced His hands and feet,
While evildoers enclosed Him.

Then "God made Him [Christ] who had no sin to be sin for us."

2 Corinthians 5:21a NIV

But sin cannot exist in God's presence!
"For You are not a God who takes pleasure in wickedness;
No evil can dwell with You."

Psalm 5:4 BSB

Thus Jesus cried out:
"My God, my God, why have you forsaken me?"

Matthew 27:46b NRSV

SUFFERING SERVANT!

"My God, my God, why have you forsaken me?"
The prophetic Psalms cried out,
"Evildoers have enclosed me.
They have pierced my hands and feet.
I can count all my bones.
They look and stare at me.
They divide my garments among them.
They cast lots for my clothing."

Psalms 22:1b, 16b–18 WEB

Gardening

"And unto Adam God said,
'Because thou hast hearkened unto the voice of thy wife,
And hast eaten of the tree, of which I commanded thee, saying, 'Thou shalt not eat of it,'
Cursed is the ground for thy sake;
In sorrow shalt thou eat of it all the days of thy life;
Thorns also and thistles shall it bring forth to thee.'"

Genesis 3:17–18a KJV

Cursed with thorns
In Eden's garden,
The Living Green also fell that dark day
With thorns scarring tender red roses
And purple thistles cursed with painful barbs,
Brambles, and briers
That need weeding daily,
Even in the tomb's garden
Of Jesus, whom Mary mistook to be

THE GARDENER!

But Jesus, whom many mistook to be a king,
Wore to the cross a crown of thorns—
Rose thorns, perhaps from the tomb's garden
That needed weeding daily
Of brambles and briers,
Purple thistles cursed with painful barbs,
And thorns scarring tender red roses,
So that the Living Green also will rise with us on that bright day
In the tomb's garden—
Blessed and dethorned!

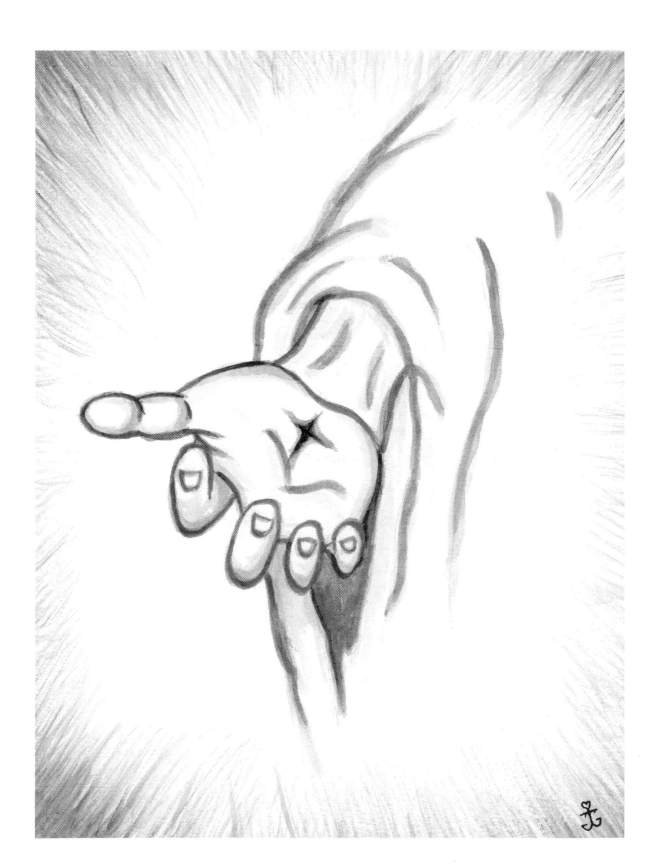

Doubting

"While the Disciples were talking about Jesus's crucifixion,
Jesus Himself stood among them and said to them, 'Peace be with you.'
They were startled and terrified, and thought they were seeing a ghost.
'Why are you frightened?' He said to them,
'Why do doubts arise in your hearts?'"

Luke 24:36–38 NRSV

Doubts that choke the proclamation of Jesus's name to all the nations!
Doubts like:
Is there really repentance and forgiveness for my sins?
Did Jesus really rise from the dead on the third day?
Is Jesus really the Messiah from Psalm 22, our Suffering Servant?
Is it now being fulfilled,
All that was written
About Him?
Or was Jesus just a ghost with no flesh and bones?
Can I touch Him and see,
See if it is the great I Am Himself?
Or maybe
Jesus lied?
How can He rise
With pierced hands and feet
From a bloody cross?

RISEN LORD!

"'Look at my hands and feet,'
[Jesus replied,]
'See that it is I myself.
Touch me and see;
For a ghost does not have flesh and bones
As you see that I have.'"

Luke 24:39 NRSV

"And He said to them,
'Thus it is written,
[And is now fulfilled!]
That the Messiah is to suffer,
And to rise from the dead on the third day,
And that repentance and forgiveness of sins
Is to be proclaimed in His name to all the nations!'"

Luke 24:46–47a NRSV

Writing Love Letters

"For I am convinced that neither death nor life,
Neither angels nor demons,
Neither the present nor the future,
Nor any powers,
Neither height nor depth,
Nor anything else in all creation,
Will be able to separate us
From the love of God that is in Christ Jesus our Lord."

Romans 8:38–39 NIV

Last Adam!

With the love of God that is in Christ Jesus our Lord,
Nothing in all Eden will be able to separate us,
For my love for you roars like nothing else in all creation.
It exceeds the mountain heights and ocean depths.
It shines brighter than the bursting of first day's light,
And greater than any power or stormy sea.
You bless me without measure, present or future.
O dear angel, see how you torture my demons
With your beckoning lips!
Oh, how your kiss caresses mine!
See how I melt into your embrace!
For I am convinced that neither death nor life—
Nor even sin—
Can shatter our love.
For truly,
Perfected in the love of our Creator
And His risen Son,
We are remade new!

Part 3

Seeing God by Helping Others

Again Jesus said, "Simon son of John, do you love me?"
He answered, "Yes, Lord, you know I love you."
Jesus said, "Take care of my sheep." (John 21:16 NIV)

Shepherding

Haiku

Howling moonless night,
glowing eyes surround lost sheep.
Lord's eyes shine brighter!

Cool morning meadow,
quenching dew beads my Bible.
His sheep drink their fill.

Wandering lamb found
in a thorn bush piercing flesh.
Our dear Shepherd bleeds!

Pasture cloaked in snow
as blue sheep shiver to eat.
His boot prints feed them!

"Feed my sheep," He said.
They can't live on grass alone—
One just ate my hat!

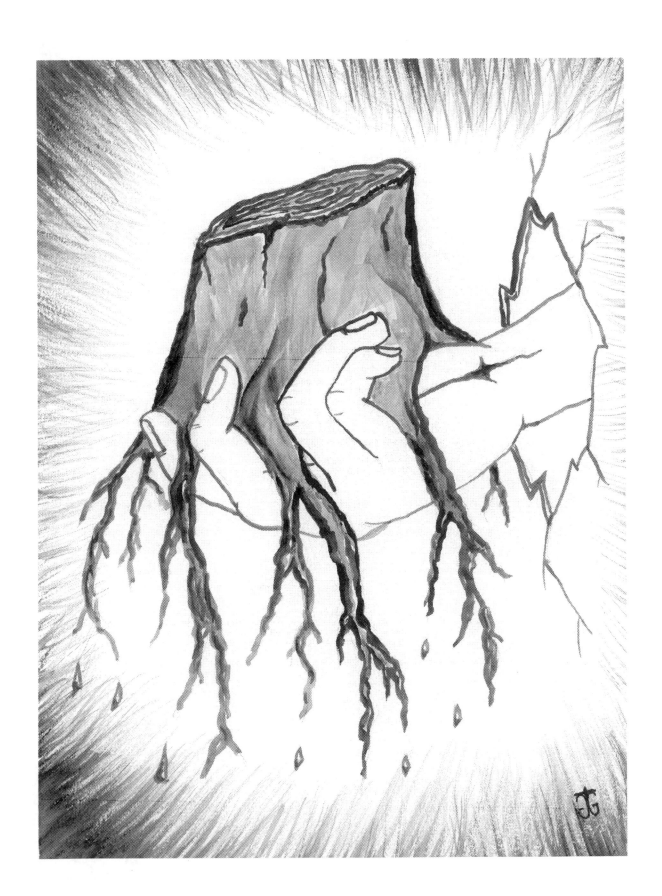

Reflecting His Love

"For now we see only a reflection
As in a mirror;
Then we shall see face to face.
Now I know in part; then I shall know fully,
Even as I am fully known.
And now these three remain: faith, hope, and love.
But the greatest of these is love."

1 Corinthians 13:12–13 NIV

HOLY ARM OF GOD!

Nothing is greater than Your love!
In the muck and mire of death and sin,
Your gifts now and forever remain: faith, hope, and love.
Even in despair, when I think I fully know everything,
I only know in part; but soon I shall know You fully
And no longer question Your mysteries.
Come sinners and stumps! Come!
"Sing a new song to the LORD,
For He has done wonderful things,
His right hand and His holy arm have gained the victory for Him."

Psalm 98:1 NASB

Truly, then we shall see You, O Lord, face to face,
Without a mirror,
Without doubting!
But for now, we see You only in our reflections,
Mirroring Your caring arms and hands,
Serving others—
Reflecting Your love!

Amen.

Returning to Eden

"A shoot will spring up from the stump of Jesse,
And a Branch from his roots will bear fruit."

Isaiah 11:1 BSB

Then
"The wolf will live with the lamb,
And the leopard will lie down with the goat;
The calf and the young lion and fatling will be together,
And a little child will lead them."

Isaiah 11:6 BSB

BRANCH OF THE LORD!

Who came as a little child, leading us
To Your cross and heaven—back to Eden!
Where the calf and lion will be together—peacefully!
And the leopard lies down with the goat—calmly!
And the wolf lives with the lamb—lovingly!
Dear Lord,
From Your Branch, help us to stay rooted in You, to bear fruits of peace,
And to spring up love from our hateful stumps.
Lead us, O Lord,
And we shall return to Eden!

Amen.

Quietly Giving

"So when you give to the needy,
Do not announce it with trumpets,
As the hypocrites do in the synagogues and on the streets,
To be honored by others.
Truly I tell you, they have received their reward in full.
But when you give to the needy,
Do not let your left hand know what your right hand is doing,
So that your giving may be in secret.
Then your Father, who sees what is done in secret,
Will reward you."

Matthew 6:2–4 NIV

RIGHTEOUS ONE!

You are my reward!
You with the Father see all secrets.
Therefore, I will shout from the mountains
And sing with the sparrows
To tell of Your overflowing love for me—and others!
How can we contain it, this flood of love?
For now through the Father's eyes I see
That my silent giving in secret
Sings the glory of Your giving!
So left and right hands, stop patting me on the back
And give quietly what is needed.
For truly, O Lord, You whisper to me that earth's full rewards
Only hide emptiness,
And that honor by others is hollow,
A white-washed tomb of shadows,
Like those hypocrites of old in their self-praising synagogues and streets.
So now, O Lord, help me to announce Your praise with trumpets
And to give to the needy in secret
Quietly, like a whisper.

Amen.

Straightening Paths

"Trust in the LORD with all your heart
And do not lean on your own understanding.
In all your ways acknowledge Him,
And He will make your paths straight."

Proverbs 3:5–6 NASB

WONDERFUL COUNSELOR!

Making our paths straight
When trails twist up and down hilly switchbacks,
And we stumble over bumps, rocks, and—sometimes—a fallen traveler,
As did the Good Samaritan,

in Luke 10:25–37

Who unlike the priest and Levite
Helped the beaten stranger.
So too in all our ways should we acknowledge God,
And like the Samaritan, praise Him by helping
And not lean on our own understanding
Of what makes a crooked path straight,
For it is Love that lifts the fallen,
When we trust the Lord with all our heart,
Straightening paths along the way
As one Samaritan helping another,
Helping another,
Helping another ...

Serving

"Jesus asked a third time,
'Simon son of John, do you love me?'
Peter was deeply hurt
That Jesus asked him a third time,
'Do you love me?'
'Lord, you know all things,' he replied.
'You know that I love You.'
Jesus said, 'Feed my sheep.'"

John 21:17 BSB

SERVING SAVIOR!

Now to us, Jesus says, "Feed my sheep!"
For today, we are His resurrected hands, arms, and voice.
You know, as we struggle to hear His shouts of "I love you!"
Tangled among the glowing walls of our online prison cells,
For You, O Lord, know all things,
And yet You still ask again,
"Do you love me?"
Why?
Why, Lord Jesus, ask a second time? Then a third time?
For as with Peter, our hearts hurt deeply
Upon hearing this question again and again:
"Do you love me?"
"Do you love me?"
"Do you love me?"
Oh, how You break—and rebreak!—our prison cells
With Your wave-pounding words.
Lord Jesus, again for a third time
You remind us to
Unplug, unplug, unplug
While helping us to find joy when we feed Your sheep.
Blazing words on our cracked, dimming screens
Beckon us to be shepherds with our
Comforting voices,
Tea-making hands,
Welcoming arms.
Serving!

Living His Love

"If I speak in the tongues of men or of angels,
But do not have love,
I am only a resounding gong or a clanging cymbal.
If I have the gift of prophesy
And can fathom all mysteries and all knowledge,
And if I have a faith that can move mountains,
But do not have love, I am nothing.
If I give all I possess to the poor
And give over my body to hardship
That I may boast,
But do not have love, I gain nothing."

1 Corinthians 13:1–3 NIV

CORNERSTONE!

If I do not live His love, I gain nothing
And crumble back into dust and decay!
For around the cross while others did boast,
Jesus gave over His body to hardship—
And death!—
So that His grace may burn within us, for truly now
If I give all I possess to the poor
But do not live His love, I am nothing.
For His grace is greater than faith, even that which can move mountains,
And greater than all mysteries and all knowledge,
And gifts of prophesy.
Yes truly, His grace does "make a joyful noise"

Psalm 100:1a KJV

Out of resounding gongs and clanging cymbals
That once did not have love
But now rejoice with the tongues of men and of angels,
Birds and beasts,
Fish and forests,
Forgiven stumps
And dandelions
Living His love!

Mirroring the Benediction

"The LORD bless you
And keep you;
The LORD make his face shine on you
And be gracious to you;
The LORD turn his face toward you
And give you peace."

Numbers 6:24–26 NIV

CREATOR!

You who give us Peace,
O Lord, help us to turn our face toward You
And to be gracious to You
And to all Creation:
The heartful and the heartless,
The blooming and the weedy.
O Lord, help us to bravely face the darkness as we shine in Your love
And to keep You
Always in our hearts.
O Lord, bless us to be a blessing.
In the name of the Father, Son, and Holy Spirit,
For Your glory everlasting, O Father.

Amen.

The Mirrors Revealed: The Names of Jesus

There are about 105 different names for Jesus referenced in the Bible. The following are used in these poems as "mirrors" to reflect God's endless love.

ALPHA AND OMEGA
Revelation 1:8 (KJV)
"I am Alpha and Omega, the beginning and the ending,
Saith the Lord, which is and which was, and which is to come, the Almighty."
("Running," page 19)

BELOVED SON
John 3:16 (KJV)
"For God so Loved the world,
That He gave his only begotten Son,
That whosoever believeth in Him should not perish,
But have everlasting life."
("Praying," page 47)

BRANCH OF THE LORD
Isaiah 11:1 (BSB)
"A shoot will spring up from the stump of Jesse,
And a Branch from his roots will bear fruit."
("Returning to Eden," page 63)

BREAD OF LIFE
John 6:33, 35a (KJV)
"For the Bread of God is He which cometh down from heaven,
And giveth life unto the world ...
And Jesus said unto them, I am the Bread of Life!"
("Prodigal Repenting," page 37)

CAPTAIN OF SALVATION
Hebrews 2:10 (KJV)
"For it became Him, for whom are all things,
And by whom are all things,
In bringing many sons [and daughters] unto glory,
To make the Captain of their Salvation perfect through sufferings."
("Smothering Fires," page 9)

CHRIST THE LORD
Luke 2:11 (KJV)
"For unto you is born this day in the city of David a Saviour, which is Christ the Lord."
("Mirror Prayer for Illumination," page xxi)

CORNERSTONE
Isaiah 28:16 (NLT)
"Therefore, this is what the Sovereign LORD says:
'Look! I am placing a foundation stone in Jerusalem,
A firm and tested stone.
It is a precious Cornerstone that is safe to build on.
Whoever believes need never be shaken.'"
("Living His Love," page 71)

CREATOR
John 1:3 (KJV)
"All things were made by Him;
And without Him was not any thing made that was made."
("Mirroring the Benediction," page 73)

GARDENER
John 20:15 (WEB)
"Jesus said to Mary, 'Woman, why are you weeping? Who are you looking for?'
She, supposing Him to be the Gardener, said to Him,
'Sir, if you have carried Him away, tell me where you have laid Him,
And I will take Him away.'"
("Gardening," page 53)

GLORY OF THE LORD
Isaiah 40:5 (KJV)
"And the Glory of the Lord shall be revealed,
And all flesh shall see it together:
For the mouth of the LORD hath spoken it."
("Fluttering," page 21)

GOOD SHEPHERD
John 10:11 (KJV)
"I am the Good Shepherd: the good shepherd giveth his life for the sheep."
("Following the Shepherd," page 29)

HOLY ARM OF GOD
Psalm 98:1 (NASB)
"O sing to the LORD a new song,
For He has done wonderful things,
His right hand and His Holy Arm have gained the victory for Him."
("Reflecting His Love," page 61)

HOLY ONE
Isaiah 48:17 (NRSV)
"Thus says the LORD,
Your Redeemer, the Holy One of Israel:
I am the LORD your God,
Who teaches you for your own good,
Who leads you in the way you should go."
("Groaning," page 7)

IMMANUEL
Isaiah 7:14 (KJV)
"Therefore the LORD himself shall give you a sign;
Behold, a virgin shall conceive, and bear a son,
And shall call his name Immanuel."
("Drawing Water," page 11)

KING OF KINGS
Revelation 17:14b (KJV)
The Lamb shall overcome them (evil kings):
For He is Lord of lords, and King of kings:
And they that are with Him
Are called, and chosen, and faithful."
("Crying Out," page 49)

LAMB OF GOD
John 1:29 (WEB)
"The next day, he [John the Baptist] saw Jesus
Coming to him, and said, 'Behold, the Lamb of God,
Who takes away the sin of the world!'"
("Ever Trusting," page 27, and "Raging," page 41)

LAST ADAM
1 Corinthians 15:45 (WEB)
"So also it is written, 'The first man, Adam, became a living soul.'
The Last Adam became a life-giving spirit."
("Writing Love Letters," page 57)

LIGHT OF THE WORLD
John 8:12 (NRSV)
"Again Jesus spoke to them, saying,
'I am the Light of the World.
Whoever follows me will never walk in darkness
But will have the Light of Life.'"
("Fishing," page 35)

LORD OF ALL
Acts 10:36 (NRSV)
"You know the message He sent to the people of Israel,
Preaching peace by Jesus Christ—He is Lord of All."
("Blooming in Love," page 13)

MESSIAH
John 1:41 (NLT)
"Andrew went to find his brother, Simon, and told him,
'We have found the Messiah'
[Which means 'Christ']."
("Branching Out," page 39)

PRINCE OF PEACE
Isaiah 9:6 (NIV)
"For to us a child is born, to us a son is given,
And the government will be on his shoulders.
And he will be called Wonderful Counsellor, Mighty God,
Everlasting Father, Prince of Peace."
("Rejoicing," page 43)

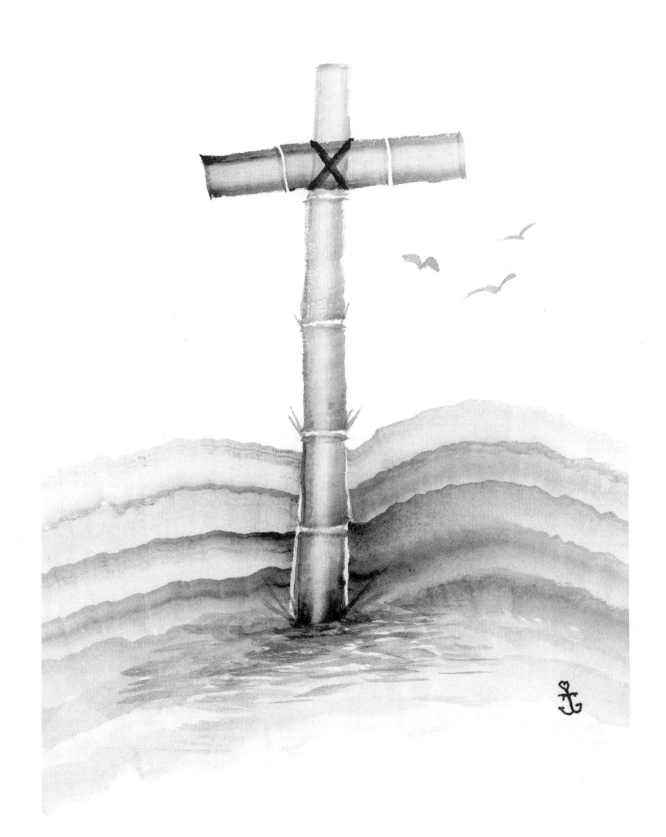

REDEEMER
Isaiah 59:20 (NRSV)
"And He will come to Zion as Redeemer,
To those in Jacob who turn from transgression, says the LORD."
("Repenting," page 5)

THE RESURRECTION
John 11:25 (NRSV)
"Jesus said to her [Martha],
'I am The Resurrection and the Life.
Those who believe in me,
Even though they die, will live.'"
("Weeping," page 45)

RIGHTEOUS ONE
Acts 22:14 (NIV)
"Then he [Ananias] said [to Saul]:
'The God of our ancestors has chosen you
To know His will and to see the Righteous One,
And to hear words from His mouth.'"
("Quietly Giving," page 65)

RISEN LORD
Matthew 28:5-6 (KJV)
"And the angel answered and said unto the women,
'Fear not ye: for I know that ye seek Jesus, which was crucified.
He is not here: for He is Risen,
As He said. Come, see the place where the Lord lay.'"
("Doubting," page 55)

SAVIOR
Luke 2:11 (KJV)
"For unto you is born this day in the city of David a Saviour, which is Christ the Lord."
("God Is Nowhere," page 3)

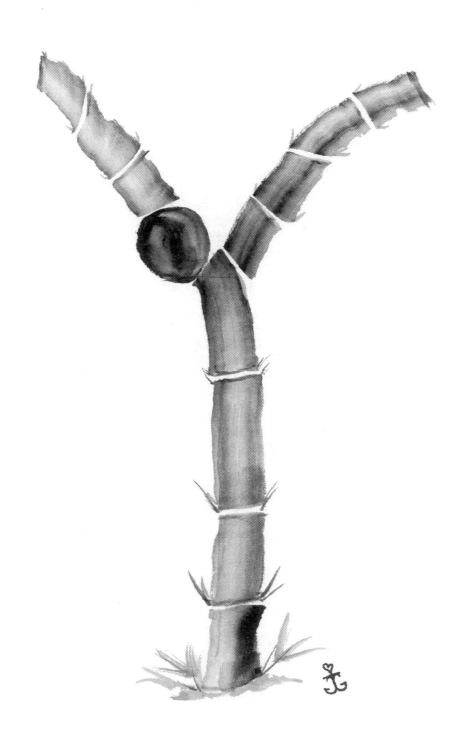

Serving Savior
Matthew 20:27–28 (NRSV)
"And whoever wishes to be first among you must be your slave;
Just as the Son of Man came not be served but to serve,
And to give his life a ransom for many."
("Serving," page 69)

Son of God
John 3:16 (KJV)
"For God so loved the world,
That he gave his only begotten Son,
That whosoever believeth in Him should not perish,
But have everlasting life."
("Embracing," page 15)

Suffering Servant
Isaiah 53:4–5 (KJV)
"Surely He hath borne our griefs, and carried our sorrows:
Yet we did esteem Him stricken, smitten of God, and afflicted.
But He was wounded for our transgressions,
He was bruised for our iniquities:
The chastisement of our peace was upon Him;
And with His stripes we are healed."
("Prophesying," page 51)

Sun of Righteousness
Malachi 4:2a (KJV)
"But unto you that fear my name
Shall the Sun of Righteousness arise
With healing in His wings ..."
("Soaring," page 23)

Teacher
John 20:16 (WEB)
"Jesus said to her, 'Mary.'
She turned and said to him, 'Rabboni!'
Which is to say, 'Teacher!'"
("Wielding the Word," page 33)

THE WAY
John 14:6 (KJV)
"Jesus said to him, 'I am the Way, the Truth, and the Life:
No one comes to the Father
Except through me.'"
("Climbing Mountains," page 25)

WONDERFUL COUNSELOR
Isaiah 9:6 (NIV)
"For to us a child is born, to us a son is given,
And the government will be on his shoulders.
And he will be called Wonderful Counsellor, Mighty God,
Everlasting Father, Prince of Peace."
("Straightening Paths," page 67)

WORD OF GOD
Revelation 19:13 (NRSV)
"He is clothed in a robe dipped in blood,
And His name is called The Word of God."
("Ever Shining," page 17)

A Quiet Calming: Thoughts for Personal Reflection and Discussion

"But the fruit of the Spirit is love, joy, peace, patience, kindness, goodness, faithfulness, gentleness, and self-control." Galatians 5:22-23a (BSB)

To help achieve a peaceful meditation on each poem, you may wish to continue with "A Quiet Calming," a breathing exercise based on the "Fruit of the Spirit." Then read that poem's reflection prompts and prayer that follow in this section.

A Quiet Calming

Slowly and deeply breathe in through your nose …
then out through your mouth …

Breathe in … hold it.
Breathe out … all of it.
Breathe in … hold it … feel it.

Now breathe out all envy …
Breathe in God's SELF-CONTROL … hold it … feel it … smile in its warmth.

Breathe out all rudeness …
Breathe in God's GENTLENESS … hold it … feel it … smile in its warmth.

Breathe out all fears …
Breathe in God's FAITHFULNESS … hold it … feel it … smile in its warmth.

Breathe out all deceit …
Breathe in God's GOODNESS … hold it … feel it … smile in its warmth.

Breathe out all cruelty …
Breathe in God's KINDNESS … hold it … feel it … smile in its warmth.

Breathe out all haste …
Breathe in God's PATIENCE … hold it … feel it … smile in its warmth.

Breathe out all worries …
Breathe in God's PEACE … hold it … feel it … smile in its warmth.

Breathe out all sadness …
Breathe in God's JOY … hold it … feel it … smile in its warmth.

Breathe out all anger …
Breathe in God's LOVE … hold it … feel it … smile in its warmth.

Reflections for "Mirror Prayer for Illumination"
page xxi

A journey of a million steps begins with one step at a time.

How can feeling exhausted and empty give more meaning to rest and your recovery of strength?

Where was God in your exhaustion?

PRAYER
Loving Father, when we feel weak, strengthen us.
When we feel dark, enlighten us.
When we feel empty, fill us;
Fill us with Your endless love, O Father.
In the name of your Son, Jesus Christ the Lord, and for Your glory.
Amen.

Part 1: Seeing God in a Weedy World

Reflections for "Gardening" Haiku
page 1

From the roaring waves to the songs of birds, all Creation glorifies God in its own way.

How does a weed like a dandelion glorify God?

How can remembering that God loves all His creations bring us closer to Nature?

PRAYER
Creating Father, help us to live together in harmony with all Creation.
Empty our selfish hearts so that Your overflowing love may fill us
And pour out through us onto all of Your creations.
In the name of Jesus, our Holy Gardener, and for Your glory.
Amen.

Reflections for "God Is Nowhere"
page 3

Our plans can wilt if we hold on to them too tightly. They need God's love to thrive.

Reflect on a time when your plans did not go as you hoped but eventually resulted in something positive. Remember, even bad times can make you stronger!

How does knowing that God sees the "big picture" in your life make a difference in how you make plans?

PRAYER

Guiding Father, help our plans to harmonize with Yours.
Strengthen our faith to trust You in all we do.
In the name of Jesus, our Savior, and for Your glory.

Amen.

Reflections for "Repenting"
page 5

Admitting one's faults can be painful yet necessary for healing. As suffocating burdens are released, God's love is finally able to enter and hold a once lost and weary heart.

What things block you from knowing God's love more deeply?

What can you do to let go of these things?

PRAYER

Healing Father, help us to "let go" of our suffocating burdens.
Find us and fill us with Your love.
In the name of Your redeeming Son, Jesus, and for Your glory.

Amen.

Reflections for "Groaning"
page 7

We are not expected to know everything, but we are expected to know when and where to go for help.

Can feeling helpless be a good thing?

How does knowing that the Holy Spirit helps us, even before we pray for help, strengthen your faith in God?

PRAYER
Ever-present Father, strengthen our faith to trust You
No matter how often we try to solve our own problems.
Help us to trust in Your love.
In the name of Your Holy Son, Jesus, and for Your glory.

Amen.

Reflections for "Smothering Fires"
page 9

Truly it is hard to be still when everything seems to be falling apart around us.

How do Bible verses like Psalm 46 give hope to our weary lives?

In your hectic schedule, when is the best time to read at least one Psalm a week?

PRAYER
Forgiving Father, smother the exhausting fires within us
So that we may live in Your peace.
Help us to find time to read Your Word and the hearts to live its message.
In the name of Jesus, our salvation, and for Your glory.

Amen.

Reflections for "Drawing Water"
page 11

It is hard to draw water to live when you are in a spiritual drought.

How do the internet, TV news, and the media in general pull us away from God?

How could you use media to bring yourself and others closer to God?

PRAYER

Saving Father, help us out of our spiritual droughts.
Enlighten us to use technology wisely,
And teach us through Your Son, Jesus,
That You are always with us.
In the name of Jesus, our Immanuel, and for Your glory.

Amen.

Reflections for "Blooming in Love"
page 13

The ways of the world are not the ways of God.

Who makes you angry?

Explain how you feel when you remember that no matter what happens, God still loves you—and loves the person with whom you're angry.

PRAYER

Heavenly Father of unconditional love,
Help us to not be consumed by anger and jealousy.
Strengthen our love to live in Your ways.
In the name of Your all-loving Son, Jesus, and for Your glory.

Amen.

Reflections for "Embracing"
page 15

In composting, discarded eggshells, plant cuttings, and dead leaves break down into usable, living soil for feeding flowers and growing gardens.

Tell of a time when you repaired something broken or discarded to make it useful again.

How does God turn our brokenness into a blessing?

PRAYER
Renewing Father, recycle and compost us.
Use our faults and failures to grow flowers of goodness,
And water us in Your life-renewing love.
In the name of Jesus, Your only begotten Son, and for Your glory.
Amen.

Reflections for "Ever Shining"
page 17

Sometimes life is a warm, calming pool, and other times it's a raging sea. The only unchanging constant is God's love.

Reflect on a time when you were afraid.

How does God help us to face our fears and overcome them?

PRAYER
Ever shining Father, help us through the dark and scary times.
Surround us in your steadfast love and keep us safe.
In the name of Jesus, Your Word made flesh, and for Your glory.
Amen.

Reflections for "Running"
page 19

Life is not a simple walk in a park. The Bible compares life to a difficult race requiring determination to obtain the prize at the end.

How are determination and rewards linked in your life?

Why does God remind us that He has a reward waiting for us?

PRAYER

Faithful Father, thank you for always loving us.

Help us to be patient and determined as we overcome our hardships

With Your Love ever running with us now and forever.

In the name of Your Son, Jesus, and for Your glory.

Amen.

Reflections for "Fluttering"
page 21

Take time to smell the roses … and listen to birds, look under rocks and up into trees.

Reflect on a time when you felt very calm and at peace with nature.

How does listening and watching our earthly neighbors bring us closer to God?

PRAYER

Father God of all creation big and small,

Help us to know Your love

By bringing us closer to all of nature, our earthly neighbors.

Bless us with the courage to care for all of Your creations.

In the name of Jesus, our glorious Lord and Savior, and for Your glory.

Amen.

Reflections for "Soaring"
page 23

Loss of a loved one can cause a person to feel lonely. Loneliness can lead to sadness, and sometimes even anger.

Reflect on a time when you helped another in their grief.

How does knowing that God is always with us strengthen your faith during difficult times?

PRAYER
Uplifting Father, help us to soar on Your healing Breath,
Your Holy Spirit, ever present.
Thank you for teaching us to love others,
Helping them through their times of grief and loneliness.
In the name of Jesus, Your righteous Son, and for Your glory.

Amen.

Reflections for "Climbing Mountains"
page 25

When we are overwhelmed with problems, it can be difficult for us to see God even though we know He is always there. Sometimes we must look to those who also love God in order to see Him.

Reflect on a time when you saw God's love reflected in others.

How can seeking out those who love God strengthen your faith in Him?

PRAYER
God of mountains and valleys,
Help us to never feel alone in our troubles
But to try to seek out those who love You as well.
And thank you for sending them into our lives.
In the name of Jesus, the True Way reflecting Your love, and for Your glory.

Amen.

Reflections for "Ever Trusting"
page 27

No sin, known or unknown, is too great for our Father God to forgive.

How do grief and anger chain us to our sins?

In times of desperation, why does remembering that God loves us help us to overcome our grief and anger?

PRAYER

Father God of ultimate sacrifice,
Thank you for breaking our chains of sin.
Help us to remember Your endless love, Your Son,
And that it was His death that sets us free.
In the name of Jesus, Your sacrificial Lamb, and for Your glory.

Amen.

Reflections for "Following the Shepherd"
page 29

For following to begin, you must surrender yourself and trust Him.

Reflect on a time when the answer to a prayer took days, weeks, or even years.

How can listening for answers strengthen your faith in God?

PRAYER

Shepherding Father, help us to trust and follow You.
Open our hearts to feel your loving embrace
As we go out into the world to reflect Your love.
In the name of Jesus, our Good Shepherd, and for Your glory.

Amen.

Part 2: Seeing God in His Loving Son

Reflections for "The Shepherd" Haiku
page 31

Joy and laughter are blessings from God.

What brings you joy and laughter?

Why are these things important for your relationship with God?

PRAYER
Smiling God of rejoicing lambs, unburden our hearts so we can laugh.
Bless our families, friends, and even strangers who make us smile.
Help us to joyfully glorify You in all we do.
In the name of Jesus, Your perfect joy, and for Your glory.
Amen.

Reflections for "Wielding the Word"
page 33

Jesus teaches us through example and parables how to love and walk together with God.

Reflect on your favorite teacher or coach.

What did this person do to become a blessing in your life?

PRAYER
Father God, thank you for all the teachers in our lives.
Bless them and keep them safe.
In the name of Jesus, our Ultimate Teacher, and for Your glory.
Amen.

Reflections for "Fishing"
page 35

Sometimes we get so comfortable living in the dark that we don't even notice it until the light comes.

What are some things that cause you to think about God?

Are there things that you can add to your life (music, books, websites, hobbies, and/or outdoor activities) to help you to think about Him more often?

PRAYER
Heavenly Father of enlightening love, thank you for walking with us
Through the dark times in our lives.
Help us to grow in your love as we learn by example
The ways of love through Your Son, Jesus.
In His name, our Light over life's dark waters, and for Your glory.
Amen.

Reflections for "Prodigal Repenting"
page 37

No matter how far away you may travel from God, He will always come running to embrace you in His love and endless forgiveness.

Reflect on something that you struggle to forgive yourself for doing.

Can asking God for forgiveness help you to forgive yourself as well?

How or why will this help?

PRAYER
Father God of broken lives, hear our humble cries for forgiveness.
Strengthen us to accept the impossible:
Your lavish, prodigal love!
In the name of Jesus, our nourishing Bread of Life, and for Your glory.
Amen.

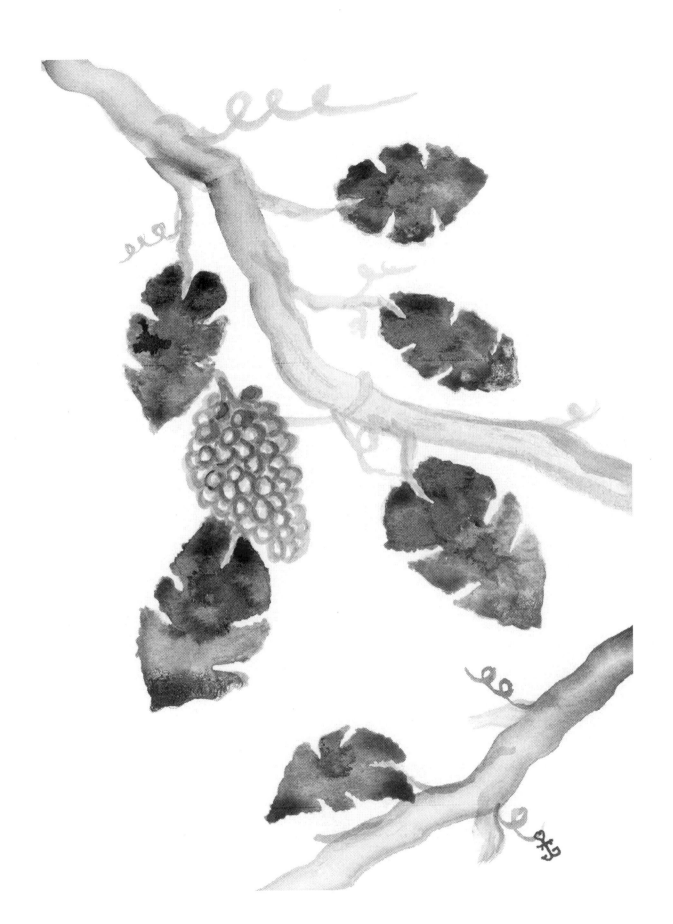

Reflections for "Branching Out"
page 39

To sculpt *David*, Michelangelo removed those pieces that weren't "David." To walk with God, we too should remove those things that aren't from God while keeping the fruit of His Holy Spirit: love, joy, peace, patience, kindness, goodness, faithfulness, gentleness, and self-control (reflecting Galatians 5:22–23a).

What do you cling to when you are stressed?

How can clinging to the teachings of Jesus relieve stress?

PRAYER
Heavenly Father of steadfast love,
Help lessen our addictions to worldly things.
Strengthen us to live by the fruit of Your Spirit.
In the name of Jesus, our Messiah, and for Your glory.
Amen.

Reflections for "Raging"
page 41

Jesus cared for the poor and needy, and so should we, for today we are His hands.

What are some ways you can help the poor?

How might you feel after you've helped?

PRAYER
Father God of raging love,
Awaken our sleepy hearts to be Your hands.
Bless us with the time and resources to be a joyful blessing to others.
In the name of Jesus, the Lamb of God, and for Your glory.
Amen.

Reflections for "Rejoicing"
page 43

God's ultimate goal, grace, is to love us unconditionally. For us, our ultimate goal should be to glorify God unconditionally. When our goals are in harmony with God's, there is peace!

What are your favorite ways of thanking God?

What are your favorite ways of glorifying God?

How is it possible to thank and glorify God in everything you do?

PRAYER
Amazing Father, as You bless us with Your endless love,
Bless also our feeble words of thanks and praise to You
So they too may be boundless like Your love.
Thank you and hallelujah!
In the name of Jesus, our Prince of Peace, and for Your glory.
Amen.

Reflections for "Weeping"
page 45

Let us not forget that Jesus, the Son of God, was also human, and as such felt peace and anger, pleasure and pain, laughter and sorrow.

What makes you sad?

What do you say to those who are sad?

What do you say when you pray for them?

PRAYER
Healing Father of sorrow and pain,
Uplift the brokenhearted,
Those feeling abandoned and tired with weary souls.
Replace their pain with Your endless love.
In the name of Jesus, our Life and Resurrection, and for Your glory.
Amen.

Reflections for "Praying"
page 47

As with any successful relationship, good communication plays a key part when talking to our Heavenly Father.

What is the difference between praying to God and talking to Him?

Could just casually talking to God improve your relationship with Him?

PRAYER

Ever-present Father of heavenly power and glory,
Help us to remember You
In all we do during our busy and hectic lives,
So that we may have a good and righteous relationship with You.
In the name of Your beloved Son, Jesus, and for Your glory.

Amen.

Reflections for "Crying Out"
page 49

Too often we try to fight our own battles, forgetting that God is always with us.

In what ways do you try to solve problems by yourself?

Reflect on a time when a problem overwhelmed you so much that you had to ask for help from a parent, teacher, or coach.

How does God help us with our earthly problems as well as our spiritual ones?

PRAYER

Father God of uplifting love,
Thank you for always being there to help us
Even when we fail to ask and try to live life on our own.
Help us to come to you even during the good times.
In the name of Jesus, our saving King, and for Your glory.

Amen.

Reflections for "Prophesying"
page 51

God is so determined to have a loving relationship with us that He sacrificed his Son to remove our sins that separate us from Him (reflecting John 3:16).

What was the best gift you ever received from someone?

How did you thank that person?

In what ways do you thank God?

PRAYER
Heavenly Father of endless gifts,
Thank you for sending Your Son to carry our sins for us.
Move our hearts to glorify You in all we do.
In the name of Jesus, our Suffering Servant, and for Your glory.
Amen.

Reflections for "Gardening"
page 53

God's Old Testament name of YHWH is unpronounceable but sounds like a breath—the breath of all living things!

How do our plant neighbors, the Living Green, praise God?

How are we connected to plants? To animals?

PRAYER
Creator God, help us to remember that all Creation is made one in Your love.
Strengthen our hearts to be the caretakers we were created to be.
In the name of Jesus, our loving gardener, and for Your glory.
Amen.

Reflections for "Doubting"
page 55

Sometimes the thing you've been searching for your entire life has been there with you all along—it just took love to see it!

What are some things you want to have faith in but find hard to believe?

How important is faith in believing in things that we don't understand?

PRAYER
Heavenly Father of doubting hearts,
Stir up our faith to trust You.
Help us to remember that nothing is impossible for You,
Even forgiving us of our countless sins.
In the name of Jesus, our Risen Lord, and for Your glory.

Amen.

Reflections for "Writing Love Letters"
page 57

One of God's greatest blessings is the love between a married couple. Thus it is no wonder that our relationship with our Lord God is often compared to that of a joyful bride and her loving Bridegroom.

How do you show your love to loved ones?

What can you do to strengthen your relationship with them?

What can you do to strengthen your relationship with God?

PRAYER
Father God, blessing us with Your endless love,
Be with our loved ones and keep them safe.
Replace our worries with peace
So that our relationships may strengthen with each sunrise.
In the name of Jesus, your sinless Last Adam, and for Your glory.

Amen.

Part 3: Seeing God by Helping Others

Reflections for "Shepherding" Haiku
page 59

Truly we are like lost sheep, seeking material things to fill our spiritual hungers.

What would you do if you won the lottery?

Would any of those things satisfy your spiritual hungers or those of others?

PRAYER
Ever-loving Father, grant us the wisdom to seek things of love,
And the gentle strength and courage to do them.
Thank you for sending Your Son, Jesus, to show us the Way
And Your Holy Spirit to guide us.
In the name of Jesus, our shepherd and friend, and for Your glory.
Amen.

Reflections for "Reflecting His Love"
page 61

Mirroring Christ's love in all we do is the sincerest form of praising God.

What are your favorite things that Jesus said and did?

How does trying to "be like Him" praise God?

PRAYER
Heavenly Father of endless love,
Thank you for Jesus and His teachings.
Help us to reflect His love to others in all we do.
In the name of Your Son, our Lord and Savior, and for Your glory.
Amen.

Reflections for "Returning to Eden"
page 63

Where we see only a dead stump, God sees new life.

Reflect on the times when you misjudged people based on outward appearances.

In Eden, what has changed so that all creatures can live in harmony? (And no, the fact that the predators are vegetarians is not the answer!)

PRAYER
Father God, open our hearts to see the needs of others
While opening our eyes to seek Your love.
Help us not to judge others but to have compassion for them.
In the name of Jesus, Your living branch from our sinful stumps, and for Your glory.

Amen.

Reflections for "Quietly Giving"
page 65

It is hard to live quietly in a noisy world.

Why does God want us to give and help others quietly?

Besides financial tithing, what other things can be given? Time? Talents?

PRAYER
Ever-giving Father,
As You have given to us
Help us also to give to others.
Hush our selfish pride so that we may do Your will quietly,
And in doing so glorify Your name, not ours.
In the name of Jesus, Your Righteous One, and for Your glory.

Amen.

Reflections for "Straightening Paths"
page 67

Sometimes the smallest seeds of kindness can grow into the largest trees of love.

What are some small acts of kindness that you have done this week?

How can these potentially grow into more kindness and love?

PRAYER
Father God of Good Samaritans everywhere,
Help us also to be kind and loving to others, known and unknown.
Empower our hearts with the courage to act, O Father,
To help others when their paths become bumpy and crooked.
In the name of Jesus, our Wonderful Counselor, and for Your glory.
Amen.

Reflections for "Serving"
page 69

Plant seeds of service to others, and you will harvest fruits of joy.

Reflect on a time when helping a stranger made you happy.

Is this happiness different from the happiness of helping a loved one?

PRAYER
Gardening Father of joyful hearts,
Open our eyes to see the needs of others,
Then water our hearts with the courage to help.
Thank you for the joy that we harvest from helping others.
In the name of Jesus, our Serving Savior, and for Your glory.
Amen.

Reflections for "Living His Love"
page 71

Strive to live like a selfless, God-filled fool, glorifying Him and reflecting His love in all things, rather than a selfish servant helping others for personal gain and cheap, hollow praise.

Reflect on a time when you did something just because it was the "right thing" to do (recited a prayer or volunteered, for example).

Did that action truly reflect God's love, or was it a self-centered personal desire to "do the right thing"?

What can you do to help weave God's love into everything you do?

PRAYER
Loving Father of the Impossible,
Help us to do the impossible!
Reflect Your love in everything we do.
We thank you for filling us with Your loving courage.
In the name of Your Son, Jesus, our Cornerstone and Rock, and for Your glory.

Amen.

Reflections for "Mirroring the Benediction"
page 73

If you are going to dance with God, let Him lead—and stop stepping on His feet!

What do you do very well? What does God do very well?

What happens when these things, like dance steps, are in harmony with each other?

PRAYER
Father God of harmony and peace,
Help us to love all
So that we may be a light to all.
Carry us through the dark and seemingly lonely times,
And help us to glorify You in all we do.
In the name of Jesus, through whom all things are made, and for Your glory.

Amen.

How to Write Mirror Poems

The beauty of a mirror poem comes from its simple but powerful reflective qualities that encourages personal inspiration. People are often moved spiritually into a deeper, more personal connection with a Bible verse or quotation when writing a mirror poem. Here are some guidelines.

1. **The Foundation.** When writing your first mirror poem, start with a Bible verse or inspirational quotation as its foundation. What is this foundation passage saying to you? How is it reflected in your life? Passages that answer questions, solve problems, or praise God are often placed in the second half of the poem. A problem can be presented in the first half with its answer reflected in the conclusion. In this case, the mirror poem is usually written from the middle out, since the foundation passage is at the end. When the poem begins with the foundation, the ending may reflect the author's personal thoughts, experiences, or spiritual revelations regarding the foundation. In either case, write down the foundation passage first, and then compose your reflective lines.

2. **The Mirror.** Be mindful of the word or phrase that is the central "mirror" and how it affects the overall theme. The mirror connects the beginning and ending of the poem. Because it is visually central to the poem, the mirror should be distinguished typographically from the other text with a different font, color, small caps, etc.

3. **Reflecting Key Words and Sounds.** Strive to mirror key words and phrases from each line of the foundation passage. Mirroring these words is essential for the essence and sound of a mirror poem. If a key word cannot be mirrored, then try its rhyming twin. To inspire you in finding the wording you want to mirror, look up different Bible translations. An online source like BibleGateway.com can greatly help.

4. **Italic Lines.** You may want to insert transitional lines that aren't mirrored to keep the poem flowing if key words aren't readily reflecting. Set these lines in italic to show that they aren't part of the mirrored structure. The main words and phrases of the foundation should always be written into the poem, but the lines in italic help make connections.

5. **Mirror-like Image.** Centering all lines of the mirror poem, including quoted scripture, and fitting them onto a single page are essential to creating the poem's mirror-like image. If your poem runs a little long, try combining shorter italic lines into a one extended line. (Altering directly mirrored lines is likely to destroy the mirroring effect.)

6. **Tips.** Reflect your favorite verses. Start short and simple. Write what you love.

Index of Bible Verses

This index includes verses that are quoted for mirroring, as well as scriptures that are paraphrased or more generally reflected in the poems. Bible verses quoted in "The Mirrors Revealed: The Names of Jesus" are indexed separately in that section.

Old Testament

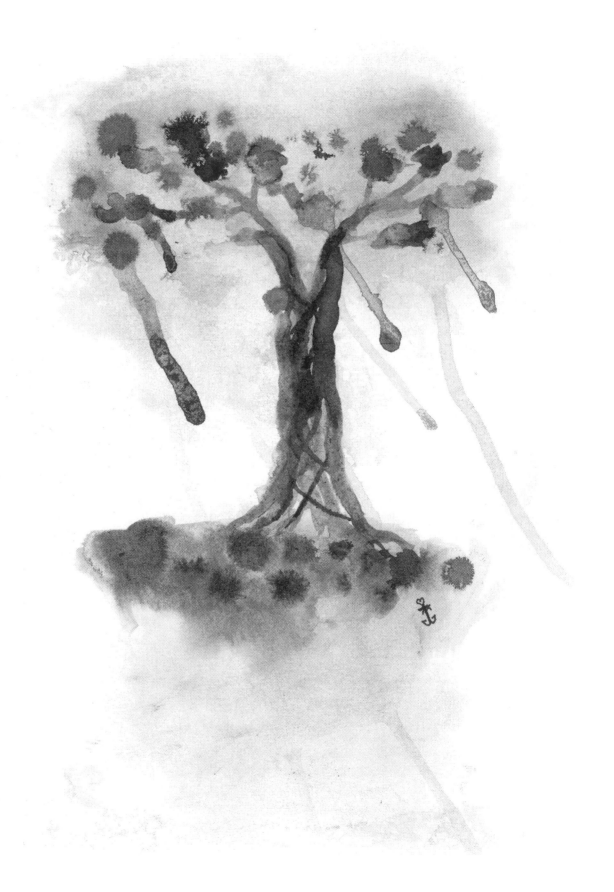

New Testament

Scripture	Poem and page number
Matthew 4:1–11 (temptation of Jesus)	"Wielding the Word," 33
Matthew 6:2–4 (NIV)	"Quietly Giving," 65
Matthew 6:9–13 (the Lord's Prayer)	"Wielding the Word," 33
Matthew 6:9–13 (the Lord's Prayer)	"Praying," 47
Matthew 13:24 (NRSV)	"Gardening" Haiku, 1
Matthew 27:46b (NRSV)	"Prophesying," 51
Mark 4:35–41 (Jesus calms the storm)	"Rejoicing," 43
Luke 5:1–11 (Jesus calls His first disciples)	"Fishing," 35
Luke 10:25–37 (Good Samaritan parable)	"Straightening Paths," 67
Luke 15:1–2, 11–32 (prodigal son parable)	"Prodigal Repenting," 37
Luke 22:39–48 (Jesus in Gethsemane)	"Praying," 47
Luke 24:36–39, 46–47a (NRSV)	"Doubting," 55
John 1:1–5 (NRSV)	"Ever Shining," 17
John 2:13–22 (Jesus cleanses the temple)	"Raging," 41
John 3:16 (KJV)	"Embracing," 15
John 10:27–28 (ASV)	"The Shepherd" Haiku, 31
John 11:21, 25–26a, 35 (raising of Lazarus)	"Weeping," 45
John 15:5 (NIV)	"Branching Out," 39
John 19:15–19 (Jesus before Pilate)	"Crying Out," 49
John 19:23–24a (NRSV)	"Prophesying," 51
John 20:15 (WEB)	"Gardening," 53
John 21:16 (NIV)	"Shepherding" Haiku, 59
John 21:17 (BSB)	"Serving," 69
Romans 5:8 (NRSV)	"Ever Trusting," 27
Romans 8:26 (NIV)	"Groaning," 7
Romans 8:38–39 (NIV)	"Writing Love Letters," 57
1 Corinthians 13:1–3 (NIV)	"Living His Love," 71
1 Corinthians 13:4–6 (NIV)	"Blooming in Love," 13
1 Corinthians 13:7–8a (WEB)	"Blooming in Love," 13
1 Corinthians 13:12–13 (NIV)	"Reflecting His Love," 61
2 Corinthians 5:21a (NIV)	"Prophesying," 51
Galatians 5:22b–23a (WEB)	"Branching Out," 39
Galatians 5:22–23a (BSB)	"A Quiet Calming," 89
Philippians 4:4–7 (WEB)	"Rejoicing," 43
Hebrews 12:1b–2a (GNT)	"Running," 19

Reflective Notes

Printed in the United States
by Baker & Taylor Publisher Services